S0-BCP-022

In the Company of Angels

Robert Strand

Volume 2

DOUBLEDAY LARGE PRINT
HOME LIBRARY EDITION

This Large Print Edition, prepared especially for Doubleday Large Print Home Library, contains the complete, unabridged text of the original Publisher's Edition.

Copyright © 2005 by Robert Strand

Unless otherwise identified, Scripture quotations are from the HOLY BIBLE, NEW INTERNATIONAL VERSION®. Copyright © 1973, 1978, 1984 by International Bible Society. Used by permission of Zondervan Publishing House. All rights reserved.

Published by Doubleday Large Print Book Club in association with Evergreen Press, Mobile, Alabama.

ISBN-13: 978-0-7394-6904-0
ISBN-10: 0-7394-6904-5

Printed in the United States of America

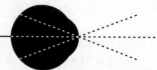

This Large Print Book carries the
Seal of Approval of N.A.V.H.

Contents

Introduction

The greatest and most authentic source of angel stories is the Bible, which contains many incidents dealing with the ministry of angels. For example, refer to Acts 12:5-11:

So Peter was kept in prison, but the church was earnestly praying to God for him. The night before Herod was to bring him to trial, Peter was sleeping between two soldiers, bound with two chains, and sentries stood guard at the entrance.

Suddenly an angel of the Lord appeared and a light shone in the cell. He struck Peter on the side and woke him up. "Quick, get up!" he said, and the chains fell off Peter's wrists. Then the angel said to him, "Put on your clothes and sandals." And Peter did so. "Wrap your cloak around you and follow me," the angel told him.

Peter followed him out of the prison, but he had no idea that what the angel was doing was really happening; he thought he was seeing a vision. They passed the first and second guards and came to the iron gate leading to the city. It opened for them by itself, and they went through it. When they had walked the length of one street, suddenly the angel left him.

Then Peter came to himself and said, "Now I know without a doubt that the Lord sent his angel and rescued me from Herod's clutches and from everything the Jewish people were anticipating."

The Bible refers to angels as "ministering spirits" (Hebrews 1:14) whom God sends as His messengers to assist people He loves. In fact, if you were to take your Bible concordance and count the mentions of angels you'll count approximately three hundred of them! It's a huge subject demanding more detailed study.

These biblical accounts cover ministry from the ascension of Jesus when two angels told the disciples, "this same Jesus" would return once again as He has gone away (Acts 1:11). An angel delivered apostles who had been arrested and placed in prison (Acts 5:19). An angel gave direction to Philip the evangelist as to where he should go (Acts 8:26). Another angel told Cornelius to send for Peter; in fact, he even gave him the address of where he was to go (Acts 10:1-6). When Peter had been imprisoned, an angel set him free, to the surprise of the church which had been praying for his deliverance (Acts 12:l-10). When King Herod failed to give glory to God, an angel brought judgment against him (Acts 12:20-23). These are just a small sampling taken from the Book of Acts.

What about verification of the angel stories of today? How do you verify the stories which appear in this book or any other book? We must depend upon the sources, the people involved. To be really candid with you, these incidents that appear in this book, cannot be documented in the same way that other miraculous events can. For example, if there is a miraculous healing, it can be documented medically. If there is a miraculous provision, it can be documented. But not an angel story. We take them at face value because we trust the source. Their appearances are usually sudden and without any corroborating witnesses in the vicinity. But the fact that something unusual has happened gives credence to the belief that some kind of an angelic ministry has occurred. If not an angel, where did the unusual help come from?

Let's have another collection of angel experiences! Let's read them with an open mind. Perhaps you will be so excited about what you read that you will share a story with a friend or neighbor. Be encouraged!

Robert J. Strand
Springfield, Missouri
2005

Dedication

To all these wonderful people
who in a step of faith and trust
have shared with us their stories.
Without you, the contributors,
this book could not have seen
the light of day.

"The very presence of an angel is a communication. Even when an angel crosses our path in silence. God has said to us, 'I am here. I am present in your life.'"
—*Thomas Palmer*

Chapter 1

THE GUIDE
FOR THE GUIDE DOG

A blind man named John who lives in New York recently acquired a guide dog named Dustin that had been bred and raised in California. Dustin had proven to be quite a capable guide dog, but he was a newcomer to Northeastern winters and their snow. During his first snowstorm, the dog became disoriented and began to have trouble functioning as they went for a walk outside John's Long Island apartment. Let's let John tell his story:

I wasn't doing too well in the snow. No one was out on the street so there were no sounds to steer me. Contrary to what most people think, guide dogs do not find the way for a blind person. The blind person really directs the dog through spoken commands.

After a very harrowing forty-five minutes, Dustin and I finally made it back to our apartment. We were safe for awhile, but guide dogs must be walked regularly, at least twice a day, which meant that later on that day we would have to go out again. I live alone with my dog so taking him out in the middle of the storm was my responsibility.

Later on that day, I was visiting with a friend on the phone. During this conversation I mentioned something about Dustin having had a difficult time in the snowstorm. My friend offered, "Next time, why don't you ask God to go with you?" So I did.

The time came for our next walk, and trusting that God would be with us, I stepped out with Dustin into the swirling snow. It wasn't long before the snow was stinging our faces, and it was difficult finding a path through the drifts. Dustin whined more than a little. "Okay, boy," I said to him, "the Lord is with us." And then I gave him a command a blind person gives only when another person is leading the way: "Dustin, follow!"

I sensed Dustin perk up and immediately he took off just like he was following someone as I had commanded. We proceeded much more easily on our walk and then headed back to our apartment.

A young woman I know who lives in our building came up and offered to walk with us to the main entrance. She said, "We'll just follow the footprints—yours and the dog's and that other person's."

How about that? Even a blind person can have an angelic encounter! Why not? Could it have been that the dog really saw the angel or just followed the tracks in the snow? Did the dog see the angel, but the kind young lady did not?

Every angel story is a fabulous experience. I marvel at the variety of ways in which these take place and the interaction between us and them. Here it seems a guide dog saw the angel. This shouldn't be hard to believe because the Bible talks about a donkey that saw an angel when his master didn't.

> *Balaam got up in the morning, saddled his donkey and went with the princes of Moab. But God was very angry when he went and the angel of the Lord stood in the road to oppose him. Balaam was riding on his donkey, and his two servants were with him. When the donkey saw the angel of the Lord standing in the road with a drawn sword in his hand, she turned off the road into a field. Balaam beat her to get her back on the road (Numbers 22:21-23).*

FOOD FOR THOUGHT: What fabulous stories! A dog follows an angel in a snowstorm, and a donkey sees an angel with a drawn sword! In each case, the humans didn't see the angel, but the animals did. You need to take the time to read the entire donkey and Balaam story (Numbers 22:21-35). Three times the donkey saw the angel and stopped, and each time she was beaten.

"Christians should never fail to sense the operation of an angelic glory. It forever eclipses the world of demonic powers, as the sun does a candle's light."
—*Billy Graham*

Chapter 2

COULD IT HAVE BEEN?

In September 1939, at the beginning of World War II, Hitler and his army invaded Poland and, in a matter of days, conquered it. Leaving Poland in ruins, the huge army of Germany moved west. The world looked on in wonder and horror. It was thought that France, with one of the largest standing armies in the world (an army of some six million soldiers), would be able to defend itself. But in ten short months, Germany had marched across France and Europe. This demoralized the Allied armies, essentially breaking the back of their resistance.

It was a discouraged and battered Allied army that stood on the banks of the English Channel at Dunkirk, France, waiting for the British to evacuate them. It was a miracle that the English were able to withdraw as many troops as they did. They used anything available that floated to bring back as many soldiers to the English shores as possible. This defeat meant much of the Allies' equipment was left behind or destroyed by the conquering Germans. England became the last stronghold of freedom in that part of the world. It looked as though Hitler would succeed in his plan to conquer Europe!

The Allied troops had no sooner safely reached British soil when Hitler called a surprise meeting of his generals, some of the best military minds in the world. He asked them to make a decision to invade England or wait for a more opportune time. When would there have been a better time? Hitler had the demoralized Allied army in his hip pocket on the verge of total defeat!

Although he knew there would have been

stiff resistance from Great Britain, Hitler thought he would be able to overcome them in a matter of months. According to conventional wisdom, there really wasn't a decision to be made.

Now here's where this story gets interesting. According to Hilton Sutton, who served in our Air Force during these events, there were a number of divine interventions during WWII, including the following incident.

At the surprise meeting Hitler had arranged, a strange "general"—not a German and not a man previously known to Hitler's staff— also showed up. This strange general persuaded Hitler and his staff not to invade England but to wait until the German army was stronger and victory was assured. It was decided the German army would invade Russia rather than England!

Had Hitler invaded England and conquered it and then moved eastward to invade Russia, the outcome of WWII could have been much different. Because Hitler and his staff of military geniuses listened to this strange general, Germany plunged into Russia ill-prepared and overconfident.

On another front, General Rommel, the German "desert fox," had General Montgomery of England and his army on the run in North Africa. Rommel's troops were poised and ready to strike the final blow to Monty's army when Hitler again called a surprise meeting of his generals. Once more, this same strange visiting general convinced them to recall Rommel to Germany and replace him with another general, who was not prepared for desert warfare. This allowed Monty time to recover and launch a counterattack, resulting in a major English victory. Then the Americans came on the scene, and Germany was in retreat.

One more time, Hitler called a staff meeting to make a major decision—whether to produce jet aircraft or continue hurling bombs at Great Britain. This strange visiting general was again present and convinced Hitler and his staff not to take the time to set up an assembly line to produce jet aircraft. By the time the Germans realized their mistake in not mass-producing jet planes, the United States had gained total air supremacy and was able to destroy most of the German industry.

Who in the world was this visiting general who continued to influence Hitler and his brilliant staff? It's believed, according to author Hilton Sutton, that nobody in the world could have pulled off such a daring feat, other than an angel! It could have been none other than "Michael," the Chief of Staff of the warring Armies of Heaven!

Hard to believe? Wait a minute! Let's look at the following verse that talks about Michael.

At that time Michael, the great prince who protects your people, will arise. There will be a time of distress such as has not happened from the beginning of nations until then. But at that time your people—everyone whose name is found written in the book—will be delivered (Daniel 12:1).

FOOD FOR THOUGHT: The archangel Michael is associated with war throughout the Bible. In Revelation 12, John writes that Michael and his angels will make war against Satan and his angels. Then there is the story in II Kings 19:35 when King Hezekiah was threatened by the Assyrians, and God sent His angel through the enemy camp and destroyed 185,000 enemy soldiers! God's special agents were on duty back there in history, why not in our modern world? You decide, was the "strange visiting general" an angel or even Michael the archangel himself?

"I believe in angels because the
Bible says there are angels, and I
believe the Bible to be the
true Word of God."
—*Billy Graham*

Chapter 3

ALMOST OVER THE CLIFF

Mayme Williams of Durant, Florida, and a coworker had a harrowing experience while they were driving through the mountains in upper New York. Mayme shares the following story:

The trip to the summit was without incident, but as we started down the other side it happened. We hit a patch of loose gravel that had somehow been dumped on top of the paved road, and our car began to skid in the direction of the precipice!

At this instant, we both saw a tall angel, dressed in white, standing on the edge of the cliff directly in front of our skidding car. The angel raised his hand with a commanding gesture for the car to stop. We knocked over the guardrail and came to a stop with one wheel hanging slightly over the very edge of the cliff. The car stopped with such a jolt that the box of cherries on the seat between us was so scattered that for weeks afterward I found some of them below the dash and under the front seat.

Of course, we were very shaken but managed to carefully get out of the car and survey our plight. My co-worker stood so gripped with fear that she couldn't move and refused to get back into the car. She was convinced the extra weight would take the car over the cliff. God gave me the courage to get in the car and back it away from the cliff. What really helped me was the angel's presence—I saw him standing in front of the car while I started it. He appeared to be holding up the right front fender and wheel.

Fortunately neither of us were hurt in any way, no bumps, no bruises, nothing, but as a reminder of our episode, the bumper needed to be repaired as well as the right front fender. The damage was so slight that we were able to continue on to our destination without any other incidents.

This same gracious lady has another angel story to share with us:

I must tell you of one more narrow escape. This happened in the Philippines while the Communists were attempting a coup. They had blockaded this particular town at both ends of the highway, and no one could get through. They laid in wait to ambush people as they traveled from Manila to the north and killed all whom they ambushed.

An angel of the Lord appeared and told me to leave this town and return to Manila and its better protection. That day as I left town for Manila, I reached the dangerous area, which was in control of the Communists. The Lord sent such a storm of rain I could hardly keep the car on the road as we traveled for miles through the guerrilla-controlled area. But when we got safely through that area, our special escort and cover—the rain—stopped as suddenly as it had started, and we arrived home safely!

In my life, time and time again, God has given us proof of the faithfulness of His promises of protection and care!

The angel of the Lord encamps around those who fear him, and he delivers them. Taste and see that the Lord is good; blessed is the man who takes refuge in him (Psalm 34:7-8).

FOOD FOR THOUGHT: What do angels do? We know they worship God and bring judgments, but they can also give us information, bring encouragement, do battle for God, and protect believers. This protection of believers may be the most common of angelic actions. What an experience to have witnessed angels in acts of protection as our two stories above have illustrated!

"The Angel who has
delivered me from all harm—
may he bless these boys."
—*Genesis 48:16a*

Chapter 4

ANGEL IN THE POOL

It was a hot, humid summer day in the Midwest. Jamie went to one of his friend's homes to spend the early afternoon in his pool. He enjoyed being with the old gang, and the swimming, diving, and horseplay was fun. After a couple hours, he reluctantly left for his summer job.

Later that evening, he had a date with Jennifer in a neighboring town. As Jamie drove home after dropping Jennifer at her house after the date, he noticed that the stars and moon had disappeared behind some clouds. The hot summer's day seemed to have permeated the night and seemingly cast a spell of darkness and humidity over the countryside. It was still hot and muggy, just perfect for a late-night swim to cool off.

As he passed his friend's home, he decided to take a midnight swim in his pool. It was late, and the house was dark. He knew that he was always welcome to use the pool at any time, but he didn't want to awaken anybody, so he quietly made his way through the backyard. While he changed into his swimsuit in the pool cabana, he imagined how good the cool water would feel on this sticky night.

Reaching the pool area, Jamie climbed onto the diving board and got into position to make his dive headfirst into the pool. As he looked down into the pool, shrouded in darkness, he couldn't believe his eyes. Beneath him in the pool was something glowing with a brilliance that was almost in the shape of a cross. Looking closer he saw something glimmering in the darkness below and thought that maybe it looked like an angel.

Never taking his eyes off the silvery, shimmering, brilliant form, he slowly climbed back down the diving board ladder and walked to the edge of the pool for a closer look. When he knelt down and peered into the pool, the glowing form vanished! It had just disappeared. He was positive now that it was an angel. Jamie peered deeper into the swimming pool and to his horror saw that there was no water in it!

When he stopped by his friend's house the next day, he learned that his friend's father had drained the pool after the guys had finished swimming in it the previous day so that cleaning and repairs could be done.

It's with fond memories that Jamie recalls this special summer night when an angel saved his life, or at the least, saved him from a life-changing crippling head, back, or neck injury.

Even though I walk through the valley of the shadow of death, I will fear no evil, for You are with me; Your rod and Your staff, they comfort me (Psalm 23:4).

FOOD FOR THOUGHT: Let's think about this interesting quote from C. G. Trumbull: "Those who are readiest to trust God without evidence other than His Word, always receive the greatest number of visible evidences of His love."

"The angels are the dispensers and administrators of the divine beneficence toward us; they regard our safety, undertake our defense, direct our ways, and exercise a constant solicitude that no evil befall us."
—*John Calvin*

Chapter 5

WOULD YOU LIKE TO
SEE AN ANGEL?

Have you ever seen an angel? Would you like to see one? How do you get to see an angel?

Dr. S. W. Mitchell, a Philadelphia neurologist, thinks he has seen one. After a long, tiring day at the hospital, he arrived home and retired early. Soon he was awakened by a very loud, persistent knocking at his door. He answered it to discover a little girl who was deeply upset.

She spoke right up and told him her mother was very sick and in need of immediate help, his kind of help. She also said he should bring his black bag along. Even though it was a bitterly cold, snowy night, Dr. Mitchell quickly dressed and followed the girl because he felt a strong urgency to help.

The little girl led him through the night to a home a few blocks away. She took him to the bedroom where a woman lay desperately ill with pneumonia. He did what he could for her at the moment and called for an ambulance to take her to the hospital. He was vaguely aware the little girl was nowhere to be seen but didn't give it much thought. While waiting for the ambulance to arrive, Dr. Mitchell complimented the sick woman on her daughter's persistence and courage to go out for help on such a terrible night.

Mystified, the woman said, "My daughter died a month ago. Her shoes and coat are still in the closet over there."

Dr. Mitchell went to the closet and opened the door. There hung what looked like the very same coat worn by the little girl who had been at his front door! The coat was warm and dry, however, and could not possibly have been worn outside in the wintry night!

One night the King of Syria sent his army under cover of darkness with lots of chariots, horses, and men to surround the city and cut off all escape routes. When the prophet and his servant got up early the next morning and checked around outside, they discovered troops, horses, and chariots all around them! The servant, obviously frightened, asked, "Now what are we going to do?"

Elisha the prophet, answered in so many words, "Don't be afraid because our army is larger than theirs!" Then Elisha prayed, "Lord, open his eyes and let him see." And when the Lord opened the young man's eyes so he could see into the spirit world, he saw horses and chariots of fire everywhere on the mountains surrounding the very army which had surrounded them!

Once more, have you ever seen an angel? Perhaps we just need to pray that the Lord will open our eyes so we can see into the "real" world all around us!

And Elisha prayed, "O Lord, open his eyes so he may see." Then the Lord opened the servant's eyes, and he looked and saw the hills full of horses and chariots of fire all around Elisha (II Kings 6:17).

FOOD FOR THOUGHT: For most of us, seeing an actual angel may never happen. In my case I have not witnessed an angel with my eyes that I know of. However, it doesn't mean that angels were not on duty in my behalf. Perhaps someday there might be a moment when all angelic activity will be revealed. But until then, we need to accept the truth that angels are real and are on guard, even when we don't see them.

"My God sent his angel, and he shut
the mouths of the lions.
They have not hurt me, because
I was found innocent in his sight."
—*Daniel 6:22*

Chapter 6

THE EMERGENCY CALL

Lou is a very busy, workaholic type of entrepreneur who also makes time in his hectic life for community service. He enjoys being a volunteer fireman because he loves to be of help, and the challenge of fighting fires had always been something he wanted to do.

That particular week had been a very busy one. He had closed his shop early on Saturday afternoon so he and his employees could kick back and relax. He had other things on his mind—his beloved team's football game. That afternoon was going to be a time for him to lean back in his recliner chair in front of his large-screen TV set and watch football for the rest of the afternoon.

Just before halftime, the phone rang, and reluctantly he picked it up. It was an emergency fire call, and he was needed immediately!

He grabbed his firefighting gear and ran out the door to his pickup parked in the driveway. He flung his gear into the back, jumped in, fastened his seat belt, and started the engine. As he flipped on his flashing emergency lights, he dropped the gear into reverse and was ready to give his truck the gas to back out.

Suddenly, there was a man standing by his open window. Lou did a double take. He hadn't seen anybody nearby when he ran to the truck. He didn't even recognize this person even though he knew just about everybody in the small town. He was a complete stranger. The man commanded Lou with authority, "Don't back out! Look behind you first!"

Even though Lou was in a desperate hurry, the urgency of the command demanded that he get out and take a look. As he opened the car door, the man completely disappeared. He had just vanished! Shaking his head, Lou put the truck in park, set the emergency brake, got out, and walked behind the truck.

Leaning against the back bumper of the pickup was a little four-year-old neighbor boy sitting on his tricycle and watching the clouds go by, completely oblivious to the world around him!

Lou was later asked, "Who do you think the man was? Where did he come from?"

Without hesitation, Lou responded, "I asked my neighbors about a stranger. Nobody had seen anyone. I just know it was an angel sent in a split second of time to save a little boy! I'm positive of it, and you'll never convince me otherwise."

"See that you do not look down on one of these little ones. For I tell you that their angels in heaven always see the face of my Father in heaven" (Matthew 18:10).

FOOD FOR THOUGHT: This portion of scripture is most often used in making the argument that we all have a guardian angel, especially little children. We can also assume a great number of God's angels are before the Father on duty 24/7 and ready to respond to any command from Him for the care and protection of these little ones.

"Angels are more fascinating than science fiction and extraterrestrial beings."
—*Mortimer J. Adler*

Chapter 7

THE SKINNY, LITTLE ANGEL

A number of years ago I was a speaker at a morning prayer group that meets in a town near Springfield, Illinois. Before I spoke, a neighboring pastor shared with us a story about his recent trip to Mexico.

Along with several others, the pastor had gone to Mexico on a preaching mission. While they were returning, their van developed mechanical problems. After jacking up the van, the pastor crawled underneath to check out the problem. Suddenly the jack collapsed, and he felt the crushing weight of the van on his chest! His companions quickly grabbed the bumper to attempt to lift the van, but they were unable to budge it.

He cried out "Jesus! Jesus!" with what little remaining breath he had. Within seconds a youthful looking man came running toward them. He was quite thin, skinny even, and small in stature. He was smiling as he approached them. When he reached the van, he grabbed the bumper and lifted the van by himself! It was as though the van was a feather in his hands.

As soon as he was freed of the weight of the van, the pastor felt his chest expand and the crushed, broken ribs immediately mend! He crawled out from under the van on his own strength.

The helpful stranger lowered the van, waved to them, and ran back in the same direction from which he had come. He simply disappeared on the horizon as they watched. No one knew who the mysterious visitor was or where he had come from!

Of all the personalities or supernatural beings written about in the Bible, it's the angels who are most constantly depicted as being identified with heaven. As you read through the Bible and study the angel stories, you will read such things as when the "angel of the Lord" called to Hagar in the wilderness "from heaven."

Then there is the time when Jacob had a vision of angels at Bethel. There he saw a ladder reaching to heaven on which the angels of God were ascending and descending. In many other places, the angels are named the "heavenly ones" or the "heavenly host."

When the angelic hosts had finished their special praises to God for the benefit of the shepherds at the announcement of the birth of Christ, it says they "went away into heaven."

*Suddenly a great company of the heavenly host appeared with the angel, praising God and **saying**, "Glory to God in the highest, and on earth peace to men on whom his favour rests" (emphasis mine) (Luke 2:13-14).*

Please note, this was not an angelic choir singing praise to God, as so many people have depicted them to be. They were "the heavenly host" appearing with the angel and speaking to them.

Another time it was an angel "from heaven" who came and rolled away the stone from the tomb of Jesus. And it was our Lord Himself who spoke often of "the angels in heaven." I trust I have whetted your appetite to make a serious biblical study of angels on your own.

Then King Nebuchadnezzar leaped to his feet in amazement and asked his advisors, "Weren't there three men that we tied up and threw into the fire?" They replied, "Certainly, O King." He said, "Look! I see four men walking around in the fire, unbound and unharmed, and the fourth looks like a son of the gods" (Daniel 3:24-25).

FOOD FOR THOUGHT: There's a traditional song that has this line in it: "All night, all day, angels watching over me, my Lord." I believe this is more than a song, it's a biblical truth that is comforting to all who might be in distress, in need, or in danger!

"I saw the tracks of angels
in the earth, the beauty of heaven
walking by itself in the world."
—*Petrarch*

Chapter 8

FOOTPRINTS IN THE SNOW

Doreene Upton of Wildwood, Florida, will never forget her experience with an angel. Along with her sister, Evelyn, age twenty-two; and Mildred Morneau, a very good friend, age nineteen; Doreene, herself only eighteen, had just finished providing the singing and preaching at a small church in Rothsay, Minnesota, in the middle of winter. Let's have her tell the story:

During the church service, an old-fashioned, white-out, blowing, drifting, Minnesota blizzard had swooped down on us. When it was time to leave, we looked out into the night. Yes, it was bad—visibility was almost down to zero. But we needed to return home to Pelican Rapids, about twenty-six miles away, so we could get ready for another engagement in Jenkins the next day.

The pastor pleaded with us not to leave in the storm, but we persisted. My sister assured him that we could make it back home no matter how bad the weather because we were "Minnesota natives" and knew how to drive in such stuff. The wind was blowing, and there was more than a foot of snow blanketing the ground with much more piling up in drifts.

Evelyn started our 1926 Dodge, and we headed for home. We drove through the snow and hit drifts as deep as the radiator cap. Soon we were bucking drifts which needed more than one attempt for us to plow through them. We stopped, backed up, and hit them again. Even though we went slowly, it was still difficult to see where the road was.

Soon we hit a drift we couldn't barrel

through, and we couldn't even back away from it. We were stuck! We eventually came to the conclusion that we had left the road and wandered into a field. We decided there was nothing we could do but have a real prayer meeting. We felt we could pray better on our knees so Mildred climbed into the backseat and fell on her knees, Evelyn and I knelt on the floorboards in the front seat, and we began to pray! I mean we really prayed! We were well aware of our dangerous situation—we could freeze; we were lost; no one would know we were missing so there was no one to rescue us. Yes, we had a real prayer meeting!

When we finished, Evelyn started the old Dodge and backed up for another run through the drift, and this time, we got through easily. But the problem remained, where was the road? Then, all three of us saw large red footprints! At first we thought they might have been left by some kind of wounded animal bleeding on the snow. But Mildred said, "No, they're large footprints!" They were bright red and we could just make them out a few feet in front of our car, illuminated by our headlights. Mildred said, "I know we are to follow them!"

And so, Evelyn slowly drove the car, following the path that the footprints had made. We hit many more drifts, but not one of them stopped us! We drove as easily as though there were no snowdrifts on the road. It was a miracle of deliverance! It was as if the road had been plowed clean even though we went through drifts that came up over the hood of the car.

What is so amazing is the footprints led us all the way home, approximately twenty miles. They led us up our driveway and all the way to our parking spot next to the humble house we were renting! When we got out of the car, we looked behind us and saw our tire tracks, but no more red footprints! Who made such huge footprints? We came to the conclusion that it was something from the spiritual world and concluded it had been an angel with huge red feet sent on a mission of mercy and help!

For he will command his angels concerning you to guard you in all your ways; they will lift you up in their hands, so that you will not strike your foot against a stone (Psalm 91:11-12).

FOOD FOR THOUGHT: It seems to me, angels must always be on duty in good days as well as bad days when the storms of life hit. Of course they are not subject to the same laws of nature that we are, so an angel who leaves tracks in the snow will not freeze to death. They are more than able to rescue us in our need, no matter what kind of day it is.

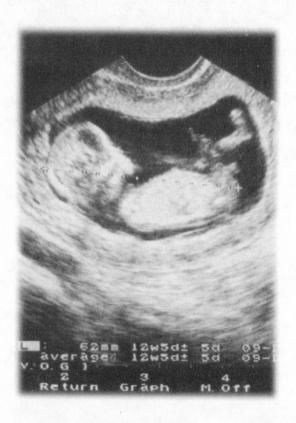

"The word 'angel' comes from the Greek word *angelos,* which is itself the translation of the Hebrew word *malakh,* meaning 'messenger.'"
—*David Connolly*

Chapter 9

THE MESSENGER

Yvonne was seventeen years old, pregnant, penniless, alone, and very much afraid. She was at her wit's end, not knowing what to do. As she sat tearfully watching the sonogram of her baby, she saw the new life moving within her and knew at that moment an abortion would be out of the question. Nightly, she cried herself to sleep.

Then, one night an angel appeared to her in a dream. He said, "Don't be afraid. Everything will be fine because you and your baby will be well taken care of."

The angel pulled back the curtain of time and gave Yvonne a look into the future. She watched as her healthy, strong, and beautiful baby was placed by an angel into the arms of a wonderful, caring couple. The next scene showed the baby as a grown young lady, mature and happy. The angel also told her God was concerned about the baby and would work everything out for good for her unborn child. Then the angel turned to Yvonne and touched her with a light that seemed to give off a warm glow that stayed in her heart during the rest of her pregnancy.

When Yvonne awoke the next morning after the dream, she felt wonderful, loved, and at peace that everything would work out for the best. Later that day she was introduced to a lady who told her about a support group home for unwed mothers, and Yvonne checked in the next day. There she found healing for her emotions and help with the choices she needed to make about her baby's future.

Her choice was to give birth and place the baby with a Christian adoption agency.

While she held her baby for the last time in the hospital, Yvonne had her own dedication ceremony for her baby. She blessed the little girl with a long life and gave her to the Lord for protection, care, and keeping.

In Yvonne's story the angel appeared in a dream with a special message just for her. There is also a biblical story paralleling hers. About two thousand years ago an angel appeared in a dream to a man named Joseph with instructions about another unborn child, and even gave him the child's name.

Later, Joseph had another dream in which an angel gave him the message to take the young child and his mother to Egypt to escape the plans of the wicked King Herod, who intended to kill the child Jesus.

The word "angel" as written in the original Greek and Hebrew language of the Bible means a "messenger" or "the messenger of God." There are all kinds of ways in which angels can get their message across to any of us in need of one.

But after he had considered this, an angel of the Lord appeared to him in a dream and said, "Joseph son of David, do not be afraid to take Mary home as your wife, because what is conceived in her is from the Holy Spirit. She will give birth to a son, and you are to give him the name Jesus, because he will save his people from their sins." All this took place to fulfill what the Lord had said through the prophet (Matthew 1:20-22).

FOOD FOR THOUGHT: W. W. How wrote: "To comfort and to bless, to find a balm for woe, to tend the lonely and fatherless, is angels' work below." Very well said! What a wonderful choice of words to describe the work of angels. Thank you, Lord, for knowing how and when to come to our aid.

"People have found that science does not have the answers for many of life's problems. While science is helpful in many ways, it just isn't enough. Humans are designed with a spiritual hunger, a sense of wonder; therefore, people have become increasingly open to the spiritual and are willing to accept the reality of angels."
—*Marilyn Carlson Webber and William D. Webber*

Chapter 10

THE TRAIN STOPS

The crack British express train raced through the night, its powerful headlight spearing through the fog and the darkness ahead. This was a special run because it was carrying Queen Victoria and her entourage.

Suddenly, the engineer saw a startling sight. Revealed in the beam of the engine's headlight was a strange figure loosely wrapped in a black coat flapping in the breeze. It looked to be standing in the middle of the train tracks, waving its arms and signaling the train to stop. The engineer immediately grabbed for the brakes and brought the train to a screeching, grinding, sparks-flying halt.

The engineer, his assistant, the coal tender, and a couple of conductors scrambled down to see who had stopped them and why. They looked all around but could find no trace of the strange figure. On a hunch, the engineer walked some yards further down the tracks. Instantly he stopped and stared into the fog in horror. The rainstorm, which had passed through the area earlier in the evening, had caused the bridge to wash out in the middle section and topple down into the storm-swollen stream.

If he had not paid attention to the ghostly, weird figure, the train would have plunged into the overflowing stream, and many lives would have been lost and bodies mangled. Who knows, perhaps even the Queen herself would have been killed or injured. The engineer was so overcome with emotion at the near miss, he sat down on the tracks for some time before making his way back to the idling steam engine.

Word was wired ahead for help. While

they were waiting for it to arrive, the crew unsuccessfully made a more intensive search for the strange flagman.

Eventually they got the train and passengers back to the station in London and solved the mystery of the strange figure. At the base of the steam engine's headlight, the engineer discovered a huge dead moth. He looked at it a few moments, and on impulse, wet its wings and pasted it to the glass of the headlamp. Climbing back into the cab, he switched on the lamp and saw the "flagman" in the beam. He had the answer now to the strange flagman—the moth had flown into the beam mere seconds before the train was due to reach the washed-out bridge. In the fog it had appeared to be a phantom figure, a flagman waving its arms signaling the train to stop!

Later, when Queen Victoria was told of the unusual happenings and the discovery of what the strange flagman had apparently been, she thought a moment or two. She declared, "I'm sure it was no accident. It was God's way of protecting us. He sent an angel in the form of a moth to warn us."

Angels come in various sizes, shapes, and forms, in whatever way we need them to come. The main thing is that God sends them for our care and protection.

> *Praise the Lord, you His angels, you mighty ones who do His bidding, who obey His word"* (Psalm 103:20).

FOOD FOR THOUGHT: If you happen to be a skeptic at heart you can shoot this story full of holes. You might say that it was nothing but a coincidence or just a chance happening. Or you can simply believe that the "coincidence" might be God at work, wishing to remain anonymous. I choose the latter. What other explanation could you put forward that makes as much sense?

"May Michael be at my right hand
and Gabriel at my left; before me Uriel and
Raphael, and above my head the
divine presence of God."
—*A Jewish Prayer*

Chapter 11

A HUGE ANGEL AT MY DOOR

Frankie Walker, a world traveler and woman minister from Springfield, Missouri, shares with us an experience she had of angelic protection:

I had just returned from five months in Israel, Hong Kong, and Hawaii. I had been invited to housesit for some friends in Tulsa, Oklahoma, while they were gone. While there, the Holy Spirit told me that I would soon be moving there and directed my thinking to a specific apartment complex. Six months later, sure enough, this came to pass, and I signed a six-month lease on an apartment.

Shortly after I moved in, the lock on the door broke, and I asked the manager if he would be so kind as to fix it. He replied, "We only do repairs if you sign a one-year lease. Or if you continue to pay month to month, we will raise the rent $66 per month and do all the repairs you need."

Being a bit short of money and not knowing how long I would be in Tulsa, I felt strongly that I should not sign the yearly lease but simply trust God for provision and protection.

This apartment complex happened to be in a high-crime area, and the door could be opened with just a slight push or a even a gentle kick. I went to bed that night praying for protection because, naturally, I felt more than a bit uncomfortable knowing how vulnerable I was in the apartment. After I fell asleep, I had a vision of a warrior angel standing outside my door and turned in my direction. He was huge! He was taller than the top of the door, which made him probably more than seven feet tall, and he was very muscular. He stood with his arms crossed and feet spread apart in a very authoritative stance.

That night I slept like a baby, and I continued to do so every night for the next year and a half. My rent was never raised, and the lock was never fixed. When I left the apartment during the day or even for several days at a time as I traveled, I never worried about somebody breaking into it. I believe the angel was there both night and day. I lived there all that time with no incident!

Then I left for Hawaii.

And that's another story. (In the next chapter we have one more angelic encounter from Frankie!)

Her word for us, which she wanted me to share with you is this: The Lord wants us to trust in Him and His protection at all times!

The heavens praise your wonders, O Lord, your faithfulness too, in the assembly of the holy ones. For who in the skies above can compare with the Lord? Who is like the Lord among the heavenly beings? In the council of the holy ones God is greatly feared; he is more awesome than all who surround him. O Lord God Almighty, who is like you? You are mighty, O Lord, and your faithfulness surrounds you (Psalm 89:5-8).

FOOD FOR THOUGHT: In all these encounters, I have discovered the angels are at work on our behalf when there is a real need! What a comfort! But remember, we are asked to trust in God, not in the angels He will send. And we are to give praise to God and not to angels when they have ministered to our needs.

"For God will deign
To visit oft the dwellings of just men
Delighted, and with frequent intercourse
Thither will send his winged messengers
On errants of supernal grace."
—John Milton

Chapter 12

A BLACK ANGEL
IN HAWAII

Frankie Walker continues with her second encounter with an angel, this time while she was in Hawaii:

While based in Oahu, a friend invited me to go with her to a street music festival in downtown Honolulu. We arrived to find a large crowd already in attendance. We were making our way from display booth to display booth, and the crowd was rapidly increasing. The crowd had quickly grown until bodies were being pressed against each other. My friend and I began to panic and looked for a way out of the crowd, which stretched from sidewalk to sidewalk. Buildings solidly lined the street with no alleys or cross streets in sight. All the buildings were closed for the evening, so there was no place to go even if we could have moved there.

We could feel panic begin to grip the crowd too. In the heat and the press, people began to faint and were carried along with the crowd because there was no place to lie down. More people were attempting to get into the festival from both ends, effectively blocking the crowd from getting out of the area. Now, I'm pretty strong for a lady and quite tall, but soon the weight of the crushing crowd unsteadied me several times. I nearly lost my footing, and to fall in this crowd would have been disastrous!

I began to pray that this crowd would not panic. I looked around and saw fear on nearby faces and felt that many people were on the verge of losing it. It was the worst mob scene I have ever witnessed. I continued to pray for help and a way out of the surging crowd.

All of a sudden I sensed I was no longer being pushed from behind or, for that matter, from either side or the front. I looked behind me and there was a tall, distinguished looking, clean-cut, well-groomed black man, with peace and calmness all over his face. He stood head and shoulders above the crowd around us. He was completely relaxed and moved with a grace that was wonderful to watch. The jostling of the crowd didn't budge him one bit. He acted as our guard so no one brushed against us! He didn't say a word, simply nodded and smiled and stayed behind us for nearly an hour until we came to a clearing and could get away from the crowd. He never moved from being our guardian during this time.

As we managed to get clear of the crowd, I turned to thank him and he was gone! Not more than a few seconds before I had looked at him. We searched everywhere, but he was nowhere to be found. He had just disappeared, but not into the crowd or we could have spotted him since he was so tall. Then I knew that he had been an angel sent to protect us.

A policeman was standing nearby and I asked him about the situation, and he said it was a miracle no one had panicked to the point of screaming, or many could have been trampled. I asked him if he had seen our "guide" and he said, "Only you two ladies."

If you make the Most High your dwelling—even the Lord, who is my refuge—then no harm will befall you, no disaster will come near your tent (Psalm 91:9-10).

FOOD FOR THOUGHT: Perhaps you're thinking, "How is it possible that Frankie can have more than one encounter with angels, and I haven't even had one?" Perhaps they have been at work in your life a number of times, and you didn't recognize their presence. In Frankie's two encounters, one appeared in a dream, and one appeared in the flesh. The Bible explains that many of us have entertained angels and not been aware of it, "Do not forget to entertain strangers, for by so doing some people have entertained angels without knowing it" (Hebrews 13:2).

"For he will command his
angels concerning you to guard
you in all your ways."
—*Psalm 91:11*

Chapter 13

ANGELS UNAWARE

Jan Winebrenner of Milpitas, California, relates the following story from the life of Dick and Margaret Hillis, who were missionaries for the China Inland Mission in the late 1930s.

In 1937 the Japanese began a full-scale invasion of China. By January 1941, the Japanese army was advancing toward Dick and Margaret's home in Shenkiu. It looked as though their city was soon to be the cen-

ter of the battle. In the midst of this dangerous time, Dick had an appendicitis attack,
and the closest doctor was about 115 miles
away. Dick and Margaret weren't sure what
to do.

Miraculously, God kept them safe, and
the Japanese did not invade the city. As
soon as he could, Dick packed their little
family into two rickshaws and headed for
Shanghai, in spite of his pain. They were
stopped at the Sand River by the Chinese
army. They asked for permission to pass
through the lines, but the commander told
them they were crazy. Eventually the commander was persuaded to give them a written note of permission to go through the
lines. As Dick and Margaret left the officers'
headquarters, they were spotted by the son
of a Christian they knew who recognized
Dick. He was an opium smuggler, the black
sheep of the family. He offered them a place
to sleep, a boat to cross the river, and a per-
sonal guide. God's second "angel" had
come to them as a smuggler.

Traveling in the "no-man's-land" between
the two forces, they were approached by
three Japanese officers. The one in the center was a two-star general. In perfect En-

glish he addressed Dick, "Where in the world did you come from?"

Dick was astonished at the man's flawless English. He quickly told his story of his illness and the need for a hospital, some help and rest, and milk for their babies. He added, "And may I ask you, sir, where did you learn such perfect English?"

Without hesitation the officer informed them he had attended the University of Washington in 1936. "General," Dick said, "please give me the pleasure of introducing you to one of your fellow alumni. My wife was also at the University of Washington in 1936."

The general's face beamed. He greeted Margaret warmly and promised to fulfill each of their requests. "In the morning, I will give you a pass to take you through Japanese lines. You will find milk at the little church, for the former missionary there owned a cow. And you shall be attended to by our medical people."

How about that? Real angels? No, not really. But people whom God used to do the work of angels. None of these three, I'm sure, were totally aware of their role in guiding one of God's servant families to safety in a great time of trouble.

The angel of the Lord encamps around those who fear Him, and He delivers them (Psalm 34:7).

FOOD FOR THOUGHT: Yes, I know, in the truest sense of an angelic encounter, this was not one of them. But why not have a story like this in an angel book? It simply illustrates another way God has chosen to bring about a deliverance. How many people in your life have fulfilled the role of an angel in your time of need? How about giving them a word of thanks? Have you ever been an angel in time of need for another?

"There is nothing unnatural or
contrary to reason about belief in angels."
—*J. M. Wilson*

Chapter 14

HOW DO I KNOW IF IT'S REALLY AN ANGEL?

Lee McGinnis of Branson West, Missouri, was unemployed and discouraged. A split-second encounter with an angel gave him just the encouragement he needed. Lee tells his story:

At that time, I was unemployed after having worked some thirty years in the same occupation. We were living on my wife's salary that she earned at a local college. This was a tough time financially for us. I had sent out résumés but had not yet received the answers I had hoped for.

One day in August I went to the mailbox looking for something, just anything by way of an answer or encouragement. The only thing in the box was an advertising flyer for back-to-school clothes for kids. By this time our kids had all left home, married, and were having kids of their own. On the way back to the house from the mailbox, about halfway up the driveway, I became overwhelmed with discouragement and stopped and looked at the flyer again. With tears in my eyes I complained, "Lord, I don't even have any kids going back to school."

At this moment in time, a young man came down the street riding a bicycle. He was dressed in bike-riding gear and looked about as normal as he could be. I didn't pay too much attention to him until he shouted at me, "Jesus! Look to the Lord, Bud!" That's all he said, and it took me by surprise. I turned to get a better look at who he was and where he was going, but he had vanished! I could see down the road a good half mile or more, and he was out of sight! He had disappeared as I watched!

What do you think? Lee McGinnis said, "I saw an angel riding a bicycle. I believe I did to this day. It was just another way for God to lift my spirits and help me to look to Him for strength and guidance."

How can you be sure if you sense or see what you think might be an angel? We again refer to the Bible for the real answers. When the angel Gabriel came to Daniel, he told him, "Therefore consider the message, and understand the revelation." Daniel, sure enough, saw the angel and heard him, but he was still required to use his own thinking powers in evaluating what the angel had told him.

This should be one of God's concepts for us in regard to what may happen in an angelic encounter. The first consideration is to regard what the Bible has to say about angels and their ministry. And the second is to place it into context with our own life experiences.

Have you been doing this as you are reading through this book? Are you really looking over these angelic encounters with your mind and with your knowledge of the Bible?

Are you prepared to do this if and when you might encounter the presence of a totally spiritual being? The Bible is also clear that we are to "test the spirits" according to the Apostle John in I John 4: 1-3.

Dear friends, do not believe every spirit, but test the spirits to see whether they are from God, because many false prophets have gone out into the world. This is how you can recognise the Spirit of God: Every spirit that acknowledges that Jesus Christ has come in the flesh is from God, but every spirit that does not acknowledge Jesus is not from God. This is the spirit of the antichrist, which you have heard is coming and even now is already in the world.

And angels are spirits! The Apostle Paul confers with this thinking, "Test everything. Hold on to the good. Avoid every kind of evil" (I Thessalonians 5:21-22).

The best test is to keep Jesus Christ front and center in your mind, soul, and spirit.

Now let me pose this question to you: What would excite you most—God's message to you or getting to see an angel?

Praise the Lord, you his angels, you mighty ones who do his bidding, who obey his word. Praise the Lord, all his heavenly hosts, you his servants who do his will. Praise the Lord, all his works everywhere in his dominion. Praise the Lord, O my soul (Psalm 103:20-22).

FOOD FOR THOUGHT: There is an observation I'm quite sure you will have to agree with: Those people in the Bible who were given the privilege of a direct visible or spoken ministry from angels are those with a mature enough spiritual attitude to want an encounter with God, not with angels. For example, Mary had a conversation with two at the empty tomb of Jesus, but when she returned to tell the disciples, she didn't say, "I have seen two angels." She said, "I have seen the Lord!" Her heart, life, mind, perspective, and spirit were right, so God was able to allow her to see angels.

"But during the night an angel
of the Lord opened the doors of the jail
and brought them out."
—*Acts 5:19*

Chapter 15

THE WARNING

It was a typical school day morning, and Ruthie Osterhus was making the regular drive with her two kids to Eugene Field Elementary School. The kids were doing their usual bickering and fighting on the short ride. This morning would be different.

Ruthie was attempting to cope with a migraine headache, and her patience was in short supply.

Shouts kept coming from the backseat,

"Mommie, he's grabbing my lunch box!" was the scream of eight-year-old Lisa.

"Did not!" shouted her nine-year-old son Tommy with just as much volume.

"Enough! Stop it!" Ruthie shouted into the backseat, "No more of it, both of you!"

It was like shouting to the wind.

"There, he did it again!" cried Lisa.

Ruthie gripped the wheel tighter, knuckles turning whiter, anger rising, but then she breathed a prayer, "Please, Lord, help me make it this last half mile."

Quietly at first, then building with each repeat came the taunt, "Lisa is a tattletale! Lisa is a tattletale! Lisa is a tattletale!"

"He's teasing me! Make him stop, Mommie!" came the cry from Lisa.

At that, Ruthie partially turned her head and scolded both of them vehemently.

Then Ruthie distinctly heard a loud voice she had never heard before. It commanded: "RUTHIE! STOP! QUICK! NOW!"

Stunned at the forcefulness of this strange voice, Ruthie quickly turned back to the road, and there was a stop sign dead ahead! It was a four-way intersection. She slammed on her brakes, and the car skidded, squealing to a violent stop. The seat belts were the only restraint keeping the kids from being pitched into the front seat or windshield.

In a fraction of a second after the stop, an old battered pickup, loaded with junk, plowed through the stop sign on her left at a high rate of speed. The driver then lost control and veered hard right, hit the curb and the truck overturned, spilling its contents all over the street!

Other motorists rushed to help the pickup driver. Ruthie, still with the steering wheel in her white-knuckle grasp, just sat there and began to shake! Another driver approached her car, and she put down the window and asked, "Is he hurt?"

"A little more shook up than anything. He'll be all right." Then he added, "Lady, I saw it all. It's a good thing you stopped when you did. That guy would have nailed you broadside. The angels sure must have been riding with you today, lady, is all I can say."

Okay, you tell me. It wasn't an appearance of an angel, so where did the voice come from? Oh, yes, the kids said they heard the voice too. What other explanations can you offer for this intervention in the normal course of human events?

Whether you turn to the right or to the left, your ears will hear a voice behind you, saying, "This is the way; walk in it" (Isaiah 30:21).

FOOD FOR THOUGHT: Well, here we are again. How do you explain such a happening? Either you believe in a supernatural intervention, or you can go on searching for a plausible explanation. Yes, I know, it does take a little bit of faith to believe angels or other supernatural phenomenon are the answer. It takes no faith to kick it all to pieces. Let's let David Ben-Gurion have the last word: "Any man who does not believe in miracles is not a realist."

"Peace is the
first thing the angels sang."
—*Pope Leo the Great*

Chapter 16

THE LITTLE
OLD LADY ANGEL

A wonderful missionary friend of ours was on a special assignment to Israel in 1990. It was during the period of time when Saddam Hussein was firing "Scud" missiles into Jerusalem as well as other parts of Israel and threatening to send many more. Naturally, people were on edge. This missionary tells her story:

A friend and I were walking through the Arab quarter in Jerusalem when one of those missiles landed near enough for us to hear the explosion. A moment later we heard another noise coming from behind us. Before I could jump out of the way, an Arab merchant with a large metal cart loaded with heavy boxes came barreling down the slightly sloped street and hit me directly in the back, just below the shoulder blades. The hit was hard because he had been running with his cart down the street. I was stunned, badly hurt, and knocked to the ground. I quickly went into shock.

Another Arab merchant helped me to sit up and assisted me to a low stool. This kind man immediately began to apologize for the recklessness of his fellow merchant. I sat for some moments attempting to gather my senses and assess the pain. I realized that I had broken ribs and other injuries.

Finally, I managed to stand to my feet with the confession, "Lord, by your stripes I am healed."

Another shopkeeper among the gathering crowd asked, "Lady, how did you manage to get back up? How are you able to stand on your feet?"

I had barely managed to remain standing because of the intense pain in my back. I suspected I also had an injury to my spine because the pain was excruciating.

All of a sudden, a little old lady, looking about seventy, stepped up to me, took both of my hands in hers, looked me in the eyes with the most compassionate look I'd ever seen, and said only one word: "Peace!" Instantly my strength returned, my knees quit trembling, the effects of the shock were gone, and all the pain completely disappeared! It was an instantaneous healing!

I turned my head to thank the kind merchant for his help while still holding the little old lady's hands, and then turned back to thank her, but she had vanished! The crowd was small and I could see up and down the street, but she was gone. She had just disappeared while she was holding my hands!

I don't know about you, but this is just another confirmation of the reality of angels. This is an interesting appearance. I've never had anyone describe an angel as a "little old lady about seventy." Well, why not?

But for you who revere my name, the sun of righteousness will rise with healing in its wings. And you will go out and leap like calves released from the stall (Malachi 4:2).

FOOD FOR THOUGHT: Do you have any friends who have criticized you for believing in angels? Don't let them bother you. You're in good company! Remember that in the Bible, the existence of angels is assumed.

"The helmed Cherubim,
And sworded Seraphim,
are seen in glittering ranks
with wings display'd."
—*John Milton*

Chapter 17

THE ANGELS OF MONS

According to this report in the *London Evening News*, Arthur Machen told how the tiny British expeditionary force, outnumbered three to one, was apparently saved during World War I by heavenly reinforcements. The "angels of Mons" and the accounts of their numbers have varied from one platoon to another as to how they suddenly took up a position between the British and the Germans. Understandably, the enemy fell back in confusion. Historically, there is much controversy surrounding the events of this story.

This battle took place on August 26, 1914, and when this story appeared in Allied newspapers in September, most of the survivors were still stationed in France. According to one account, a British officer said that while his army was in retreat from Mons, a unit of German cavalry came charging after them. The British ran for a place from which to make a last stand, but the Germans got there first. Expecting almost certain death, the British troops turned and saw, to their astonishment, a troop of angels between them and the enemy. The German horses were terrified at the sight and stampeded in all directions.

Later, a British army chaplain, the Reverend C. M. Chavasse, recorded that he had heard similar accounts of the miraculous Mons angelic deliverance from a brigadier general and two of his officers. A lieutenant colonel also described how he, too, during this retreat, watched as his battalion was escorted for about twenty minutes by a host of phantom cavalry.

From the German side came a confirming

account that their men refused to charge a certain point where the British line was broken because of the presence of a very large number of troops. According to the Allied records of this battle, there was not a single British soldier in the immediate area.

This is one of those historical stories having many versions, some denials, and few plausible explanations. About the only thing we know is that something miraculous and unusual intervened in this battle of August 26, 1914.

This particular story has been around for a long time and is one of those that is still very controversial. What is quite noteworthy about these accounts is that not one of them is reported firsthand. In each case officers and soldiers wished to remain anonymous because it might hinder any future promotions they were in line to receive. In other words, there was no one bragging about it to gain any fame whatsoever.

So we can continue with speculation about the reality of what really happened. One of the things of interest to me is that none of the officers or soldiers involved wanted to be identified with the story because it might have an effect on how they would be perceived. I've also found this to be the case in many stories of angel encounters today. Many people have volunteered their story with this reservation: "I have had this experience but have never told anybody because they might think I'm nuts." But they have shared it with me, apparently because they perceive me as someone who will not ridicule them. This is one of the reasons I have changed the names in many of the stories or in other ways disguised the identity of the people.

God is a righteous judge, a God who expresses his wrath every day. If he does not relent, he will sharpen his sword; he will bend and string his bow. He has prepared his deadly weapons; he makes ready his flaming arrows (Psalm 7:11-13).

FOOD FOR THOUGHT: Think with me about the military aspect of angels. It's evident that a large part of their work is warfare. Why? Because God is a warrior God. "The Lord is a warrior; the Lord is his name" (Exodus 15:3). Yes, God is a warrior and He wins every battle! Therefore, when angels engage in warfare, they too never lose!

"Angels descending, bring from above,
Echoes of mercy, whispers of love."
—*Fanny J. Crosby*

Chapter 18

WHAT POLICEMAN?

The Curtis Steen family from Idaho was traveling on I-35 through Iowa in a typical winter snowstorm. As they traveled, the storm increased in its fury. Travel was slow and harrowing in the blowing and drifting snow. They decided to keep on going so they could reach their destination on time. They were also hoping they would be clear of the storm by the time they reached the Missouri border.

But of real immediate concern to them at the moment was the gas gauge in their car—it registered empty! They had stopped in a couple of towns only to find the storm had closed down everything, including gas stations. The only solution was for the family to begin praying for help.

It became absolutely critical that they find fuel, or they would be stuck out on the road in the storm. At the next small-town exit, they turned off and went again in search of help. A police officer pulled alongside their car and motioned them to lower their window. He asked them if they needed anything.

Curtis replied, "We're just about out of gas." The officer told them to follow him to a gas station to which he had a key, and he would help them get some gas, even though it was closed.

They followed him and fueled up their car. When they went to pay him, he refused their money. Relieved to have gas once again in their car, they drove off. They had not gone far when Lou Ann spoke up from the backseat, "We didn't thank the man for his help." In their rush to get back on the road, they had neglected this courtesy, and their little daughter reminded them.

So they turned around before they reached the highway and drove right back to the station, only to find that it must have been abandoned for years. Now they were really intrigued and mystified.

They decided to track down the police officer who had helped them. They drove around without any success until they stopped a man who was out on his snowmobile. They told him they were looking for the town cop, who had been so helpful to them, because they wanted to express their thanks before getting back on the interstate.

The snowmobile rider told them the town had never had a cop before and certainly did not have one now.

What an exciting story! The more I collect, catalog, interview, research, and write angel stories the more intrigued I am about the fabulous variety and endless opportunities in these encounters. Think about this miracle. Where did the gas come from? Where did the electricity come from to pump the gas into the tank? Where did the policeman come from?

How did the car materialize, the one he

was driving? How did the abandoned station come back to life for those few moments? And how did the angel learn how to drive a car? All I can say in response to these and more questions is to use the word that lots of young ones use: awesome!

Jesus did many other miraculous signs in the presence of his disciples, which are not recorded in this book. But these are written that you may believe that Jesus is the Christ, the Son of God, and that by believing you may have life in His name (John 20:30-31).

FOOD FOR THOUGHT: I think a quote from the pen of Hope MacDonald has a thought for those of us who may have never encountered angels: "We may not experience the supernatural deliverance of an angel, but God promises us supernatural strength of spirit." If angels are part of our miraculous deliverance, wonderful! But what if angels don't appear? Simply remember, God has always promised His presence with us. Angels are wonderful, but God is greater!

"A guardian angel
o'er his life presiding,
Doubling his pleasures,
and his cares dividing."
—*Samuel Rogers*

Chapter 19

SHORT STORIES ABOUT ANGELS

Angie grew up in one of those small towns along the Mississippi delta. She was eight years old, and one of her duties was to walk home from school every day with her six-year-old brother. The best part of this daily walk down the tree-lined street was to pause in front of one of those beautiful, southern, large brick houses with pillars out front. The gardens were gorgeous and surrounded by an ornate wrought-iron fence, painted white.

On this particular afternoon, as they paused to enjoy the mansion before them, she and her brother felt a hand on their shoulders, lifting them and gently placing them about fifteen or twenty feet away. At the same instant, a speeding car, careening out of control, jumped the curb and smashed into the iron fence, at the exact spot where they had been standing! When Angie and her little brother had recovered, they turned around to see who had picked them up. No one was to be seen!

In her book *A Slow and Certain Light,* Elizabeth Elliot relates an experience her father had:

My father, when he was a small boy, was climbing on an upper story of a house being built. He walked to the end of a board that was not nailed at the other end, and it slowly began to tip. He knew he was doomed, but inexplicably, the board began to tip the other way, as though a hand had pushed it down again. He always wondered if it was an angel's hand.

The cancer had been marked by pain and suffering. Joan's mother was in the last few hours of life. On this night, Joan was seated next to her mother's bed, and they had been quietly remembering many of the happy events of life they had shared together.

Suddenly, her mother sat bolt upright in bed and with an expression of joyfulness said, "I can see my mother and father!" She paused, waited, then excitedly said, "I can see Jesus!" There was another pause, and then she said, "He's motioning for me to come! And, oh, Joan, I see the most beautiful angels!"

With this beautiful look of radiance on her face, she laid back on her pillow and quietly passed from this life. Joan said, "The room seemed to be bathed in peace."

During World War II, James was a crew member on a B-29 bomber. They were flying over a part of central Europe on their way to a target in Germany. As they were making their final approach to the assigned target area, he felt a strong hand on his shoulder and a voice commanded: "Get up now and go to the back of the plane!"

Immediately after he had made his way to the back of the plane, they came under a limited antiaircraft attack. James waited until it had died down and sensed it would be safe to return to his seat in the front of the plane. When he returned, he noticed three shells had blown holes in the ceiling of the plane. They had entered from the bottom and penetrated through his seat and out the top! His confident explanation is simply that an angel had been sent to warn him.

It was a tragic night in an inland Chinese city. The bandits had come and surrounded the mission compound, which sheltered hundreds of women and children. On the previous day the missionary, Miss Monsen, had been put to bed with an attack of malaria.

She had prayed: "Lord, I have been teaching these people all these years that Your promises are true, and if they fail now, my mouth shall be forever closed and I must go home."

The next night, she experienced a healing in her body and was up among the frightened refugees who had come for shelter from the terrorists. She encouraged them to trust in God and pray for deliverance. The raids continued all around them, but the compound was untouched by violence.

In the morning, people from three neighboring families asked Miss Monsen, "Who were those four people, three sitting and one standing, quietly watching from the top of your house all night long?"

Last night an angel of the God whose I am and whom I serve stood beside me and said, "Do not be afraid, Paul" (Acts 27:23-24).

FOOD FOR THOUGHT: Billy Graham supplies this food for thought: "As an evangelist, I have often felt too far spent to minister from the pulpit to men and women who have filled stadiums to hear a message from the Lord. Yet again and again my weakness has vanished, and my strength has been renewed. I have been filled with God's power not only in my soul but physically. On many occasions, God has become especially real and has sent His unseen angelic visitors to touch my body to let me be His messenger for heaven, speaking as a dying man to dying men."

"I saw the angel
in the marble and carved
until I set him free."
—*Michelangelo*

Chapter 20

WHAT DO ANGELS
LOOK OR SOUND LIKE?

The well-known artist Rockwell Kent was hosting an exhibition of his paintings. Quite a crowd showed up, and of particular interest were his paintings of angels. The artist was making his way through the crowd, answering questions, meeting people, and explaining his works.

He came upon a lady who had been staring intently at one of his celebrated angel paintings. Spotting the artist coming toward her, she turned to him, pointed to the picture and exclaimed, "No angel ever looked like that!"

To which the artist, without emotion asked, "Have you ever seen an angel, Madam?"

From the Bible and in any number of the stories in this book, we have seen that angels can take all kinds of forms, visible as well as invisible.

But what does an angel sound like? What specifically does an angel say? Based on the little research I've done on the subject, I have discovered that many times an angel's voice sounds remarkably like someone saying, "Hurry up!"

We tend to think that angels speak in beautiful, softly spoken, well-modulated tones. But the words, "Get up!" are rarely wonderful, especially at 5:30 A.M. Yet, as you study the Bible, you will discover the angels are constantly saying, "Hurry up! Get up! Get going!"

With the dawning of the day, angels urged Lot, "Hurry and get out of this place! Take your wife and your two daughters" and leave!

An angel prodded Gideon with, "Rise up and get going!"

An angel said to Elijah, "Get up and eat!"

An angel appeared to Joseph in a dream when Herod was killing all the infants and said, "Get up! Take the child and his mother and escape to Egypt!"

An angel (it may have been the same one) appeared in another dream to Joseph in Egypt and said, "Get up! Take the child and his mother and go to the land of Israel."

Angels met the women at the empty tomb of Jesus and said: "Go quickly and tell His disciples!"

An angel made an appearance to Philip and said, "Get up and get going!"

An angel appeared in a jail cell and told Peter, "Get up, quickly!"

An angel said to John when he fell at his feet to worship him, "Do not do it! Worship God!"

Really, angels seem to say the same thing over and over. Maybe there's a message there for us—not to waste our time, but to be about our Father's business.

When the angel of the Lord appeared to Gideon, he said, "The Lord is with you, mighty warrior" (Judges 6:12).

FOOD FOR THOUGHT: It doesn't really matter what an angel looks like or how an angel sounds, but it is important what an angel has to say. In this book we've seen angels assume all kinds of appearances. It seems as though their physical appearances are in tune with the type of surroundings they're in. I'm just thankful that God has created angels to worship Him and minister to humans in need!

"The angels come to visit us, and
we only know them when they are gone."
—*George Eliot*

Chapter 21

DO ANGELS KNOW CPR?

It was a cold early December night in 1990 when Douglas Craig, newly trained and graduated from the police academy, was on duty. He had been assigned to work a patrol at the Denver Airport. Making his rounds, he started down a long, deserted walkway. Quite a ways ahead of him, he watched as an older man stopped, collapsed, and slumped to the floor against the wall.

Doug ran quickly to help the man. He was

doing his best to try to remember his training as he reached to check a pulse and
found none. The man had also stopped
breathing.

This was Doug's first emergency, and he
was alone with no backup. He immediately
called for medical help on his police radio.
The sterile classroom training he had recently taken seemed so long ago. He
sensed that if he didn't do something
quickly, the man would die before help arrived. What could he do? He breathed a
prayer, "Jesus, please help me. Help me to
know what to do."

Just then, coming from behind him, he
heard a woman's voice saying, "I'm an emergency room nurse. I'll do the chest compres-
sion if you will do the CPR breathing."

Doug wondered where she came from.
He hadn't heard any steps behind him or
seen anyone coming down the walkway.
The floor was hard-surfaced, so any steps
would have been heard from a long way off,
echoing off the hard surfaces of the walls
and ceilings as well. Shrugging off his questions, he focused on the task at hand.

Doug began the mouth-to-mouth CPR,
while the nurse did the chest compressions.

When the paramedics arrived and took over, the man began to revive.

"Then," Doug says, "the most peculiar thing happened. I stood up and looked around for the nurse so I could thank her, but she was gone! No one was there! The walkway was long, and no exits were handy. She should have been easily seen. She had appeared out of nowhere when I desperately needed help, and when the crisis was over, she had simply vanished!"

Do you think angels know how to perform CPR? Would an angel have to resort to CPR to revive someone?

To this day, Douglas Craig believes angels know CPR—well, at least one of them who took the form of a woman and appeared out of nowhere when she was needed in Denver.

As a policeman, to this day, Doug is one cop who always makes his patrols with a sense that there can be divine help in times of real need.

And my God will meet all your needs according to His glorious riches in Christ Jesus (Philippians 4:19).

FOOD FOR THOUGHT: Here's something to think about—angels never die! Therefore the angels we will meet in heaven will be the same ones we have read about in the Bible. Think of the excitement in meeting Gabriel and Michael and the one who shut the mouths of the lions in the den for Daniel. What about the one who rolled away the stone from the tomb of Jesus? Then we will want to meet the angel who led Peter out of jail and many more. Angels will always be only angels for all of eternity. And God will always be God throughout eternity!

"See that you do not look down on
one of these little ones. For I tell you
that their angels in heaven always
see the face of my Father in heaven."
—*Matthew 18:10*

Chapter 22

ANGELIC PROVISION

Jonathan remembers well his angelic encounter even though it happened more than seventy years ago. He was ten years old, and the Depression of the 1930s was at its peak. He had younger brothers and sisters, and it was one difficult struggle simply to keep food on the table for the family.

Being the oldest child, one chore assigned to Jonathan was to do the shopping for his mother every Saturday. He would hand the list to the grocer, who would help pick out the items. With money in such short supply, this was a highly trusted job for such a small boy, but he did it with pride and a strong sense of responsibility.

On this particular Saturday morning, his mother gave him the grocery list, tucked $10 into his jacket pocket, and sent him on his way. She always warned him never to buy anything that was not on the list. When the proprietor had loaded his wagon with the groceries from the list, Jonathan stopped at the counter to pay the lady at the cash register. She asked him for $9.74. He reached into his jacket pocket, and there was no money to be found! Frantic, he searched through every pocket in his pants and through the jacket again, but he could find no money! He pulled off his shoes and socks thinking it might be there. He looked under his cap; he ran back through the store hoping to see it on the floor. No money! The grocer went through his jacket pockets. Nothing! He began to cry. There was nothing to do but leave the groceries and go home to tell his mother.

Of course, she was angry and upset. To lose $10 in those days was a near catastrophe. There would be nothing for them to eat that week beyond what had been left in the cupboards. It was a bleak prospect.

Having done everything he could to find the money, Jonathan crept into the basement to cry. Even though he was only ten, he knew what this all meant. As he was sobbing, he heard a strong, positive, but kind voice coming from behind him. The voice called him by name, "Jonathan, just look into your jacket pocket."

How strange, he thought. He'd been through the jacket at least three times, the clerk at the grocery store had been through his jacket, and his mother had gone through it a number of times. But he stuck his hand into the pocket to feel for the money once more and satisfy the voice. And there, inside the pocket, he found the wadded-up bills—$10 in all!

To this day, more than seventy years later, whenever discouragement strikes, Jonathan still remembers the time in the basement when God heard the cries of a little boy and sent a messenger to put $10 into an empty jacket pocket!

I never get tired of listening to or recounting angel stories. Each is different and unique, but all show the goodness of a loving God to His children when in need. What encouragement and hope they bring!

However, as it is written: "No eye has seen, no ear has heard, no mind has conceived what God has prepared for those who love him" (I Corinthians 2:9).

FOOD FOR THOUGHT: Have you ever questioned, "Why study or read about angels? What's in it for me?" We need to understand by faith that angels may be watching over us, ready to come to our rescue and serve the Lord as they serve us. The realization of this truth is more than comforting, it will assist us in living out lives that give praise to God.

"The angel of the Lord appeared to her
and said, 'You are sterile and childless,
but you are going to conceive
and have a son.'"
—*Judges 13:3*

Chapter 23

THE ANGEL PROMISED

Samuel Doctorian is an Armenian, born in Beirut. He became a Christian in Jerusalem as a teenager. He's a fascinating man who shares his story of conversion as he travels in places such as Lebanon, Israel, Egypt, Jordan, Syria, Greece, and Cyprus. The following is his exciting story:

One night while sitting around their kitchen table, James Osmand and his wife Liberty shared with me their sorrow at losing three children. And the saddest part, Liberty shared with tears, was that doctors now had said there was no hope for them to have another child.

She said, "I'm so sorry I've lost three, but the worst is I will not have any more children. I'd love to have another child."

Of course I felt compassion and prayed with them. Then about eleven o'clock, I retired for the night. I got ready to go to bed and fell on my knees to pray. As I was praying, suddenly an angel of the Lord came and stood right in front of me in the bedroom! I saw him in full bright light. He had a glorious face and a wonderful smile. He came with a scroll in his hand and did not speak. He opened the scroll, and I read the words from the Lord. It was a clear message: "Go and tell my daughter, I shall give her a son next year."

You can imagine my joy and excitement. I quickly put on my robe and ran downstairs. They were still in the kitchen talking together and weeping. Jim was trying to comfort his wife.

I came in with great excitement and said: "Liberty, I have a message for you. The Lord just now sent an angel to my room."

She shouted: "What? An angel? Right here?"

I said, "Yes. He just came in my room while I was praying. And this is the message, Liberty. 'Next year at this time you shall have a son.'"

Can you imagine the tremendous joy of that night? I don't remember what time we went to bed, but we all rejoiced and praised the Lord for this glorious message that the angel had brought.

Oh, yes, you must also know this, exactly one year later—to the day—a son was born to James and Liberty Osmand!

Awesome! The story doesn't end there. Eighteen years later I was in England attending a "League of Prayer" convention with Jim Osmand, who was one of the special speakers. Liberty and Jim were happy to see me, but their greatest joy was for me to meet their son, the promised one. He was eighteen years old and a very dedicated Christian. How thrilling it was to see him, hug him, and praise God for the glorious and wonderful fulfillment of the message that the angel brought to me in the upstairs bedroom, eighteen years before! Hallelujah!

In the sixth month, God sent the angel Gabriel to Nazareth, a town in Galilee, to a virgin pledged to be married to a man named Joseph, a descendant of David. The virgin's name was Mary. The angel went to her and said, "Greetings, you who are highly favored! The Lord is with you." Mary was greatly troubled at his words and wondered what kind of greeting this might be. But the angel said to her, "Do not be afraid, Mary, you have found favor with God. You will be with child and give birth to a son, and you are to give him the name Jesus" (Luke 1:26-31).

FOOD FOR THOUGHT: Why not another announcement of a pending birth by an angel? Think of some of these same kinds of announcements in the Bible—an angel announced the births of Isaac, Samson, Samuel, John the Baptist, and of course Jesus Christ, as well as others. Can you imagine the excitement in the hearts of the parents who received such news? You may be thinking, "I'm not ready for such news! Or, I'd like to meet an angel, but with a different message." Well alright, or maybe this, too, would be your heart's desire.

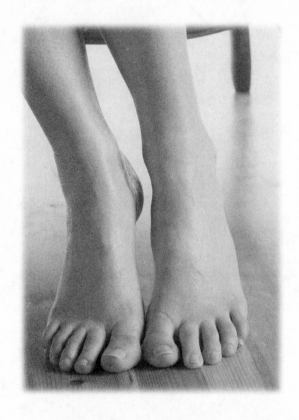

"The angel of the Lord
encamps around those who fear
him, and he delivers them."
—*Psalm 34:7*

Chapter 24

SARAH'S ANGEL

Sarah recently had a nightmarish experience and lived to tell the story. She was returning to her car, which was parked in the mall parking lot when she was accosted by two men, who forced her into their car at gunpoint. They blindfolded her, tied her up, and hurriedly drove out to a deserted stretch of woods where they raped her. Before her attackers left, one of them pulled out a pistol and shot her three times, and then they both fled.

Several hours passed; she had no recollection of how many, but somehow she started to revive. She managed to struggle to her feet and futilely searched for her shoes but couldn't find them. In her bare feet she stumbled, fell, crawled, and walked out to the country road. She knew if she was to have some help, she'd have to walk the many miles to town. With her goal in focus, she began to make her way on the harsh, sharp gravel of the roadway, stopping frequently to rest. She began to walk and fall, then sat for a while to gather strength until she could get up to proceed. She began to fear she would die before she found help.

She prayed and asked God to please send someone to help her. Nearly delirious with pain and the loss of blood, she suddenly felt like she was being helped along. It was almost as though she was carried, and she didn't stumble or fall anymore. Quickly she reached the first home on the edge of town, and at that moment, it seemed to her as if she were placed gently back on the ground.

There was a light on in the house. She managed to walk up the three steps onto the porch and knocked on the door. A young woman answered, took one long look at Sarah, and crumpled to the floor in a dead faint. Her husband stepped over his wife to help Sarah inside to a couch on which to lie down.

He quickly phoned 911 for an ambulance, then went back to help his wife who was beginning to revive. When the wife felt better and was seated in an easy chair across from the couch, Sarah managed a weak, wan smile and whispered, "I'm sorry that I frightened you like this. I know I must look terrible."

The wife replied, "No, that's not why I fainted. I saw this great big shining angel holding you up as you stood in the doorway!"

Later at the emergency room of the hospital where the ER doctor examined her, he noted that even though she had covered several miles on the rough gravel road, there was not even one scratch or bruise on her bare feet! Further, he couldn't understand how the three gunshot wounds had closed up so she didn't bleed to death, and there also seemed to be no internal bleeding or injury to her organs. In fact, after a night's rest and stitches to close the wounds, Sarah was able to walk out of the hospital under her own power and return to her normal life. She had completely recovered from her ordeal!

The Egyptians mistreated us and our fathers, but when we cried out to the Lord, He heard our cry and sent an angel and brought us out of Egypt (Numbers 20:15-16).

FOOD FOR THOUGHT: Most everyone knows something about angels, well, at least at the sentimental level through greeting cards, songs, and poetry. But are angels real? Perhaps we should have asked this question at the beginning, but why not here? For most people the answer centers around how they view the Bible. The Bible plainly states: Abraham, Jacob, Moses, Joshua, Gideon, David, Elijah, Zachariah, Joseph, Mary, Peter, and many others all saw angels. Is this enough proof for you? Have these very human stories in this book convinced you? In order to believe, you need to have some measure of faith.

"Do not forget to entertain strangers, for by so doing some have unwittingly entertained angels without knowing it."
—*Hebrews 13:2*

Chapter 25

THE HITCHHIKER

While doing research for this angel book, as with others in the past, I've come across one type of angel story that seems to occur quite frequently. Practically every publication about angels has some version of a "vanishing hitchhiker." The details may vary from version to version, but the overriding theme is constant. The following are a couple of these stories.

Pastor Davidson was on his way to make a call on a sick member of his Colorado church. He had to travel about fifteen miles on a desolated stretch of barren land to reach their ranch home. He stopped to pick up a young hitchhiker, which is a common courtesy in the country. As they drove along, the pastor began to share with the young man about the love of Jesus Christ.

Pastor Davidson specifically said in the course of conversation, "I believe the Lord's return is getting very close."

The young man softly, yet forcefully, replied, "Well, that will be sooner than you think." The boy's reply was a surprise to the pastor.

They drove further, and the young hitchhiker continued, "Please make sure you are ready and that all of your congregation also gets this warning."

The pastor now contemplated this message, sensing that some kind of special occurrence was happening. He drove with this eyes on the road.

But when the pastor next turned to look at his passenger, the young man was gone! The pastor stopped the car, got out, and looked up and down the lonely stretch of road but was unable to see anyone in any direction!

Here's another story, this one about the encounter that Matt had with an angel. He was driving along a state highway on his way to the next appointment when he saw a hitchhiker out in the middle of nowhere. He stopped to let the nice young man get in. The man immediately began to talk about Jesus Christ and the goodness of God the Father. He urged Matt to prepare himself for the days ahead in which he would pass through a special test of his life. They discussed having a relationship with Christ and also about the future.

Matt looked away to check the road ahead, turned back, and the passenger was gone! Curious, he stopped in the next town at the police station to report on the missing hitchhiker. The police sergeant on duty replied, "You're the fifth person to stop by today to tell us about a vanishing hitchhiker matching the description you've just given me."

Do you think the frequency of this kind of story could be a message to all of us who may be living in what may well be called "the last days"?

The Son of Man will send out His angels, and they will weed out of His kingdom everything that causes sin and all who do evil (Matthew 13:41).

FOOD FOR THOUGHT: Does God always use angels to get his message across? No. God could do it all Himself without using angels, nature, other people, or any kind of phenomena. Or God can use angels as messengers to accomplish what He wants. God is God and is not limited by any one method. He may use an angel one time, but a word from a stranger the next time. Or He may give us help in finding a lost item by a thought or through gifts of food from a neighbor! It's an exciting adventure serving God! We never know what God might do next in our lives. However, we should not stop praying for His help and His guidance.

"What he did see was light:
light from the Heavenly Host
as they swept the sky clean from
one end to the other."
—*Frank E. Peretti*

Chapter 26

THE LAST WORD OR TWO

How does a contemporary person living in the twenty-first century deal with anything called supernatural? Are you comfortable with this spirit world of angels we have been recording? How do you explain such phenomena contained in this short book? We have more than twenty-five factual events involving angels interacting with human beings.

The truth of these stories depends upon

the veracity of the folks who have been willing to share them with me and, consequently, with you. Many of these have never been told before. I have not researched any of these accounts beyond receiving the story from the people who have experienced them. These must be taken at face value as they have been shared.

The larger question is what you are doing about these incidents presented as fact. It's okay to be a critical reader, but at some point you must deal with deciding the truth—angels are either real or simply a figment of someone's overworked imaginations. You be the judge. As for me I believe angels exist, and they can appear at any time in a person's life to help or minister to human need.

Billy Graham states, "Angels have a much more important place in the Bible than the devil and his demons!" True!

There are two very important things to keep in mind when dealing with angels. First, at no time should an angel or angels be worshiped! Never. The Bible is very clear on the fact that only God is to worshiped!

Second, we are not to pray to angels. You might pray and ask God for help in an emergency, but never pray directly to an angel. All prayer is to be directed to God and to His Son, Jesus Christ, not to angels. We need to open our minds to understand and ask God to help us develop a healthy balance in regards to His angels.

No one knows how an angel looks, but by the fourth century, artists began to depict them with wings. Then, by the twelfth century the debate raged as to whether they were male or female. Martin Luther and Calvin both believed in angels, but Luther prayed so God wouldn't allow any angels to appear to him in any dreams because they were distracting to his work.

Angels still remain a mystery, and if you read the Bible and do an in-depth study of angels, you will have more mysteries. Based on what we have seen, angels appear suddenly; they serve a myriad of purposes; they can assume different appearances, and these appearances are usually fleeting. Perhaps after reading through this book, you are left with more questions than answers, and that's okay. But now, you just can't ignore them!

The stories here have depicted many kinds and types of angelic encounters with human beings. To the best of my knowledge, all the people reporting such sightings have been believable. They have given testimony to a real happening. You, the reader, will make your own interpretation. Some of you have been entertained, some have been challenged, some of you are still as skeptical as you were when you began reading, and some of you have, in faith, taken these stories and given praise to the God who created them! You have rejoiced in the awesomeness of God. You have blessed the Lord God Almighty for His wonderful works among the people of this world.

The angel said to me, "These words are trustworthy and true. The Lord, the God of the spirits of the prophets, sent His angel to show His servants the things that must soon take place" (Revelation 22:6).

FOOD FOR THOUGHT: Has this been a complete anthology? No! My desire is that this has stimulated you to become a student of the Bible and a student of the God of the Bible. Although angels are not the

Bible's main theme, they are part of God's creation. May your studies draw you ever closer to the Creator of the universe and the Author and Perfector of our faith!